SURE, WHY THE HELL NOT.
YOU ONLY LIVE ONCE

BY JON ROBERT QUINN

Introduction

Sure, Why the hell not. You only live once. That is what we should all be saying every single day, every single time we are presented with a challenge or idea. In life we tend to make excuses for ourselves. We say things like, "it's ok" or "maybe another day" or "It's too hard" or "it's too expensive" or "I can't do that". And what's happening is, we are closing off our minds to ever accomplishing anything of meaning or quality or even things we want in life.

I had been throwing the idea around for about a year or so to write this book. I have had the title and the cover all ready for the publisher and even at one point started marketing that the book was coming but the words were stuck in my head and I wasn't motivated to get them onto paper. I have been talking about writing this book for months and I'm not sure if I was procrastinating, making excuses for myself or even just too busy, but the bottom line was, I wasn't getting it done. Now, for the people who know me, I am not a lazy guy and when I say I am going to do something, I tend to get it done quite quickly. Let me rephrase that. I am actually a pretty lazy guy, but not lazy in a bad way. I would rather work smarter than harder. It makes more sense for me to create something once that will make me money for years than get up and go to a job every day to make just enough money to get me to next month to have to do it all over again.

Currently, I am working on a variety of projects. I have The Cold Call King book series which has done quite well. I am shooting video for my YouTube channel. I am recording new shows constantly for clients in the community. I have my music career, writing and producing records and putting on concerts. Most of my time these days are spent building my Streaming TV Network JRQTV. I have a lot of irons in the fire and writing another book wasn't much of a priority because it doesn't produce a ton of money in comparison to my other endeavors. So, why am I writing the book now? Because I finally had some time off and and said to myself, "Sure, why the hell not."

As kids

When we were kids, we were fearless. We tried everything and weren't afraid of much. We were afraid of the dark, monsters, clowns, vegetables... things like that. Me? I was afraid of jump rope, being cool, getting beat up, you know, the usual. I grew up in poor neighborhoods and usually was the odd man out. Most of the kids in my neighbourhoods were the kids of gang members or their folks were incarcerated. If you're not familiar with where I grew up, you can look it up. I grew up on the streets of Tennyson Road in Hayward, California and San Pablo Ave in Richmond, California. I was one of the only white kids in primarily ethnic neighborhoods and I was a skinny, dorky kid with glasses and Kmart shoes. That should sum it up.

I remember in fourth grade, one of the kids asked if I wanted to jump rope. I was terrified that the rope would hit me in the head so I didn't. I would instead get on the roof and throw rocks or shoplift. Where were my parents? That's a discussion for another book. I had few friends and got into a lot of fights. I was also a runaway as I grew up in a very abusive house. It was so abusive, I still have nightmares to this day.

When it rained, my friends and I would cut class and go swim in giant puddles on the baseball field or the creek. They were sometimes two or more feet deep and was a way we would rebel. In high school, I started riding BMX bikes and the trend continued. I would cut school on rainy days and do the same thing I did as a kid, except now on construction sites, ghost riding my bike into the giant flooded holes the construction crews left behind. Why am I telling you all this? Because we were fearless as kids. We did what felt good and at the time, we didn't think about consequence. It's kind of like when kids do something wrong and then later are asked why did it and don't have an answer. It just felt right. It was fun in the moment. And the hell with consequences.

I am not saying to not think about the consequences. But if you want to be anybody in this world, you have to quit second guessing yourself and put yourself out there. What will your world will come to if you don't take the opportunities presented to you?

When Obama announced he was running for President, he was the underdog with no support and no money. With a little hard work, he found support and found investors and since he had a vision, he made his mark. Was I a supporter of Obama? Am I a supporter of Trump? I'm a supporter of the leader of our nation, whoever they are. This is my country and I support our leaders.

Sure, Why the HELL Not

What about Will Smith when he got the role for Fresh Prince? He was broke living with his girlfriend and she told him to go to The Arsenio Hall Show. He was already a recording artist but his last album was a flop and was broke. He was riding the bus. He was THAT broke. He shows up to Arsenio's show and was invited to a party later that evening. Quincy Jones was at that party and offered him a role for a show but would have to audition at that moment. He asked if he could prepare and come back next week for the audition. Due to scheduling, that wasn't an option. He was forced to audition in that moment at that place with those people present. Talk about nerve wracking. He nailed the audition and signed the contracts in a limo parked in front of the party and the rest of it is history.

The lesson here? Seize these opportunities and quit making excuses for yourself.

Opportunities

What are opportunities? The definition of opportunity is: a set of circumstances that makes it possible to do something.

Let's break this down. It's an event that presents itself at a certain moment in time that presents a change for the person the opportunity presents itself to. Does that make any sense at all? I'll explain it a different way.

You're at work and you're sitting next to your co-worker. There's a promotion coming up and both of you want it. Only one of you will get it and maybe only one of you are qualified for it. You both apply and you get the job, BUT you have to still decide if you want to take the offer because you will be moved to a different office and will have to travel. There's a pay raise involved but the time and travel expense may eat at the increase of money you'll receive and you also may be categorised in a different tax bracket too, in turn bring you less money. BUT, it sure would look good on your resume.

There's a lot of variables here. For one, your co-worker was also presented with the opportunity but she wasn't qualified. So, was it an opportunity at all for her? I would say that it wasn't. She had no chance because she wasn't qualified. So many times, we think an opportunity is an opportunity when it actually isn't. Now in this circumstance, you were given an opportunity and you have to decide if you want to take it. There's a pay increase. Your resume is improved. You are given new challenges. The problem is, so many people see the challenge and shy away from the idea and would rather stay in the same place. I see this over and over again.

This is one of those moments you say, "Sure, why the hell not." When opportunities like this present themselves, you should take the job and work out the details as they present themselves. This is what will help you grow. You have to step outside of your comfort zone or you'll be stuck in the same place forever.

We see this in relationships all the time. One person is abusive. It could be verbally, emotionally, sexually, or even a drug or alcohol abuser, but instead of improving their situation, they just stay in the situation, remaining unhappy. In recent research exploring women's decisions about whether to stay in or to leave their relationships, the single most important determinant of women's decisions to remain in their relationships was relationship satisfaction.

Buying My Motorcycle

When I was a kid, both of my uncles rode motorcycles. I got to ride with them and it was one of the only memories I have as a child that I cherish. The smell of my uncles cigarette smoke blowing in my face. The cars all around us in traffic. The smell of the motorcycle exhaust. The sound of the engine revving. The smell of the old Shoei helmet that he no longer wore. The cold on my skin as we rode to the store to get more egg nog. It's the simple things in life we cherish.

I would ride on the back of my uncle's motorcycle from age six or seven until my teen years when my father bought a Yamaha Vmax. If you're not familiar, the Vmax is literally one of the fastest, most bad-ass bikes built in the 1980s. That design lasted until the mid 2000s. The design changed very little and was one of those bikes that made you drool over the idea of riding a bike one day. I remember when I was maybe 15 or 16 years old, I would walk to my girlfriend's house and pass by a Yamaha dealer and would always walk in and sit on the bikes knowing that when I got my license, I would buy a bike of my own.

I am still a huge fan of that bike to this day. What an amazing machine. 1200cc, 140 hp and under 600 lbs. Just a fast ass bike with a lot of balls. My dad went crazy and bought a bunch of cool helmets and gloves, and leather this and leather that. I was about 15 at the time when one day I was at the motorcycle shop and I saw this awesome helmet. It was about $100 at that time. This is the 90s. It was quite expensive. I was at the shop and was looking at a brand new red Yamaha R1. I told my dad when I get my license, I'm going to get, "that bike right there. The red one." I bought that helmet that day with the dream of it matching my new motorcycle when I become of age. My logic was, I could wear it on dad's bike when I ride with him until then. He didn't mind because he had really expensive helmets and didn't want me scratching them.

Years would pass and I kept that helmet on a shelf always waiting for the time I would buy my red Yamaha R1. The story goes, I graduate from high school and move to central California with my mom and took the helmet with me. It sat there on the shelf waiting. It waited all the way into my twenties when I sold the helmet never buying a bike. Why didn't I buy a bike? For one, I couldn't afford it. But could I really not afford it? I think it was fear. Fear or crashing. Fear of getting hurt or even killed. I would have nightmares of crashing a motorcycle and seeing myself flying through the air and into on coming traffic. Sounds pretty logical but how many people actually get into accidents of this magnitude?

Sure, Why the HELL Not

When I was around 25, I started a fund in a little envelope in my kitchen called the GRAM fund. This is an absolutely true story. GRAM stood for Get Rob a Motorcycle. I found this little 250 cc Kawasaki at the motorcycle dealer for about $2500. That was a ton of money for me at the time. I would put $100 here and $100 there and I think the envelope got to maybe $800 before I gave up on my dream once again. Why was this? Was I still afraid of crashing? I think I took the money and put it toward a cheap red Mazda Miata. I paid around $2000 for this car and it was a heap of crap, but it was my heap of crap. I loved that car. My motorcycle dream fizzled once again.

Let's fast forward to my mid-thirties. I am now married, have my shit together. My finances are in order. I have good credit. I am a local celebrity working on national fame. My book The Cold Call King is a Best Seller. I'm building talk shows at a local radio station and playing guitar in a band. I walk into a Harley Davidson dealer because I need a wallet with a chain for when I'm on stage performing with the band. We're jumping around and being rock stars and the last thing I need is my wallet falling out of my pocket into the audience. That would not be good. As I am walking into this Harley dealer, there's a matte black Harley Iron 883 sitting by the door. I was blown away. What a sexy bike this was. I'm not a big guy so those big full dressed bikes just don't do it for me. I throw my leg over the bike and wow, it felt so good. I ask the sales guy the price and he says it's under $9000. I grab my phone and send a picture to my wife. Her response blew me away.

Moments after sending my wife a picture of this bike on the showroom floor and spending $50 on a wallet, my wife sends me a text back with, "Nice. Get it." The ball is in my court. Here's another opportunity. We talked about this earlier in the book. The wife approves. My credit is good. I'm in love with the bike. I can afford it. The price is good. I tell the sales guy I want to think about it and I leave the store with my wallet with the chain and head over to band practice.

That night I talk to the wife and she tells me I have always wanted a bike, so get the bike. I hesitate. Is it because I'm chicken or afraid of crashing? A few days later we're in Vacaville and pass a Harley dealer. I pull over to show the bike to my wife in person. I cannot believe she's all for the bike. This is something that could kill me. Well, so can cars, and everything else in this world, right? We walk up to the bike and she was impressed. It fit my frame. It made me happy. It fit our budget. We proceed to discuss terms and financing and in fifteen minutes, we were the owners of a brand new Harley Davidson. One problem though. I had never ridden a motorcycle. I didn't have a license to ride a motorcycle. And I didn't even know how to start a motorcycle. I had always ridden bitch... or as a passenger, and didn't know the beginning of ownership of a bike.

There were nights I would dream about riding my motorcycle on the freeway and crashing. I would see myself flying and falling and feel the devastation. Those nightmares haunted me for years. Then throughout the day, I would see bikes out and about and would gravitate toward them. There's a passion that runs in us that is in our blood. I would see guys with helmets and think they were so cool and so brave because they overcame whatever fear they had, and followed their passion.

As we live through life, we cannot let fear control us. It will cripple us. But it will also keep us alive. When riding, if you're not in fear of falling, your odds of an accident are much higher. If you're a business owner or professional of something, if you fear a task, operation or challenge, that will keep you from excelling in that profession. We, as humans have to continue to challenge and scare ourselves if we are going to grow.

Motorcycle Training Classes were a trip. I had to start at the beginning and I remember riding the coned track and switching from 1st gear into 2nd and into 3rd and being so blown away that I was fulfilling a life long dream. After the three day course, I get my certificate and head down to the DMV for my license. A few days after my license came, the motorcycle was delivered to my front door. I was in awe. This was mine. All I had to do was take the leap of faith and listen to my heart. Had I walked on the opportunity, I would still be wondering what it was like to finally own my bike.

The story gets funny from this moment forward. The first day riding on my new bike, somebody runs a red light and had I not taken my motorcycle training classes, I wouldn't have known proper procedure in this situation and would have been killed. I identified the driver in my mirror, saw he wasn't stopping and coming up behind me. My feet and hands were in the proper position and dumped the clutch. The bike moved from a dead stop, over about 6 feet and the truck blew right through the red light where I was sitting. After several close calls and thankfully no accidents, I traded the bike in for a brand new Mercedes SUV for my wife's birthday that year. I made a decision to ride, accept the responsibilities, evaluate the situation and moved on with my life. My father also sold his bike.

In life, we are handed opportunities and we have to decide if it's right for us or not and sometimes, it's best to just say, "Sure, why the hell not" and sort through the events that follow as they are presented. But as I said before, if we don't take the leap of faith, we never grow as person, husband, parent, friend, business owner, or whatever. We have to challenge ourselves to grow.

Buying My First Porsche

Over the years, I have had many Porsches but the story of how I purchased my first Porsche is actually quite funny. This was maybe a decade before I bought my Harley. I was in my mid 20s and was trying to get my shit together. I had a business that was doing pretty well. It was definitely a challenge. Tell me one business that isn't though. If you think running a business is easy, then you're lying to yourself because it's a constant struggle as markets and client needs change. Okay, back to my story.

I was doing a lot of buying and selling at the time and one night, my girlfriend at the time and I were at a Target and she approaches me says, "why are these speakers so cheap?" They were Sony speakers with a subwoofer for $11. I went to management and he said that was the correct price. I pulled them up online and they were around $79 everywhere else so I bought every pair they had. I went back day after day, buying everything they had and would be waiting as they unloaded the truck. Over the course of a couple months, I purchased a total of 84 pairs of those speakers. I was then taking them out to the flea market and selling them for $50. Not a bad mark up.

In the meantime, I am taking all of my profits from the speakers and placing it in my safe and one day, I am on Craigslist and this Rainforest Green 2001 Porsche Boxster pops up and I was in love. I had always wanted a Boxster. When I was in High School, the Porsche Boxster was released and my father and I went to the dealership to check it out. So all these years later, here I am with cash burning a hole in my pocket and there's an opportunity to buy my first Porsche. I felt so rich and in a way, I was because I was doing this for me. There are so many people in this world that play it safe, and that's dangerous. We only live once and we have to accomplish our goals and do things for ourselves otherwise, why are we here? To satisfy others? We need fulfilment and this Porsche was my reward for all of my hard work.

I walk into the dealership to look at the car and took it for a test drive and I had to have it. I was in love. The sound. The power. The feel. The smell. There is something about a Porsche you don't get from any other car manufacturer. The salesman and I sit down and work out the numbers and he asks how I would like to make the down payment. I tell him I will paying cash. He didn't think I would be paying in $20 bills. I tell them I need to get my cash out of my safe. They thought I was balking. I was far from balking. I absolutely wanted that car. I told them to get it into detail and I would be back in an hour.

I drive home, grab my cash and throw it into the bottom of an empty box and fill the box all the way up to the top with cheap sunglasses I would sell at the flea market. Walking back into the dealership and into finance was priceless. I walk in and he asks if I have my cash. I take the box and pour maybe a hundred pairs of cheap $5 sunglasses onto his desk and sitting on the top is $5000 in $20 bills wrapped $1000 at a time. All the sales guys walk in and are like, "I want some" and start trying on sunglasses and taking what they want. The finance guy takes the $5000, seals it into the envelope and starts prepping the contracts. I had an opportunity and took it. I could have balked and walked. I could have said, it's too expensive. I could have made excuses and never taken the leap to buy a high end sports car. Ironically, the maintenance on that car wasn't bad at all. It broke a couple times over the years but was relatively inexpensive to fix. Since then, I have had two more Porsche Boxsters and would buy another one in a second. In my opinion, it's probably the best sports car ever built.

Getting into Radio

A lot of you may or may not know, I was at one point a national radio host on radio stations all over the country. This all started on accident. Or was it? I was a mortgage loan officer. I have talked about my story getting into mortgages in other books so I won't cover that here, but what I will cover is HOW I got into radio.

I had just been fired from my latest mortgage gig and was pretty happy about it. I was building Awepra.com now known as JRQTV and was ready to take this idea to the next level. When I was at Paramount Equity Mortgage, I would be building my platform on one screen and writing loans on the other screen. Most people were struggling to meet their numbers at work and I was not only #1 in the company in production, but I was also building my company at the same time.

I was now working at this shit hole mortgage company called Trinity Mortgage making half the money I was at Paramount Equity and was pretty sick of the bullshit there and one of the other agents was calling on my leads and I walked into the boss' office and told them to do something about this "clown that's stepping on my dick." I was fired that day. Good riddance.

Two weeks later I'm at Starbucks pitching advertising to somebody for Awepra.com and a gentleman walks over and tells me I should be building a radio show at a local station. Two things happened here. Opportunity #1 was him walking up to me and pitching me and the irony is, he was fired a week later because of poor performance. Apparently I was his only client in four months at the company. Opportunity #2 was that I took his offer and ran with it. This was exactly what I needed to take my career and company to the next level.

As we get older, our brains become a lot more comfortable with familiar patterns and routines. They become less agile and flexible. Neuroscience tells us that it becomes increasingly difficult to break out of existing mindsets. As a result, habits are formed which lead to rigid thinking.

When we look at the nature of habits, many of them are the result of a desire to avoid the repetition of a mistake. It's dumb to settle into a habit based on fear. A flexible mindset that thinks outside the box might look at a mistake as an opportunity to learn and not something to be avoided in the future. Flexible mindsets can seize opportunities because it always collects and processes new information.

Three weeks to the day after I met the gentleman from the radio station inside Starbucks, I launched The Good Life Show with Jon Robert Quinn on Money 105.5 fm. I was told by everybody that I would fail and would be out of business within six months. Ten months later, I was voted #1 FM radio in Sacramento. Shortly after, I launched shows in Seattle, Denver, and Miami as well. Within a couple years, I had over a dozen shows and was making insane money. I was making more money than I ever made at any other point of my life. And then I started getting stupid and bought everything whether I could afford it or not.

POOR

They say the acronym for POOR is Passing Over Opportunities Repeatedly. As I have grown as a business owner and mentor, I have coached hundreds of business owners and usually the ones that take my advice typically do pretty well and the ones that don't, well…. they usually fail.

The saying goes, "You can lead a horse to water, but you can't make them drink". This is so so true in business. Small business owners typically become business owners because they don't want to answer to bosses anymore and want to do their own thing and though the ideology is correct, they forget that their clients are their bosses now. Not only are their clients they boss, but there are protocols in business to ensure success. One of these protocols is taking opportunities that are presented to them. People are not dealt the same hand in life. They all have different starting points.

We are all born with different talents and abilities. However, we all have the choice to get better at what we do and, despite our starting point in life, we can often do something about it — to either get ahead, stay still, or slide backwards.

I prefer to view success in life as a choice. But I know many people who see things differently. Some people attribute the success of others to luck, circumstances, connections, and even family ties. These people are free to think that successful people are successful because of luck, but if that's how they want to view the world, then they haven't really explained why successful people are successful. They've only given an excuse for why they are not.

The bottom line is that successful people have made it because they had an opportunity and they made the most out of it. We all get at least one chance to make it big in life. Some people refuse the opportunity, some people don't recognize the opportunity, and some people *waste* the opportunity. So let's discuss what that means and how it relates to where you are in your life and what can you do to make things better.

I could be sitting at work right now in a cubicle waiting for my next break and texting my friends about what we're doing tonight and instead I am writing a book. This book will not only inspire others but it helps grow my brand and takes my company to another level and it also creates more residual income that will help me retire early. And as I continue to create more and more intellectual properties that generate revenue, I get richer and people will continue to tell me how lucky I am. I'm not lucky. I just got tired of working for the man and I also got tired of working for clients so I continue to create new products and I monetized my business and intellectual properties. Basically, I automized my business. THIS is how you get rich and you have the same opportunities I do.

A lot of people waste their opportunities in life by refusing to work hard. They get offered an opportunity and start working at it but they quickly get tired. They start thinking that their opportunity doesn't have much potential. They believe their opportunity will not lead to the future they desire. And they accordingly let go of that opportunity.

That usually happens when the opportunity comes and they're not prepared for it. They slacked off in the past. They didn't invest in themselves and their abilities. And now they don't have what it takes to take full advantage of the opportunities coming their way.

Some trivialize the opportunity. They think that working on their writing skills, communication skills and taking classes is not worthy of their time. They make fun of those that go to public speaking classes. They make fun of those that go to writing classes or marketing classes or business classes. They think such skills aren't necessary for success.

Average people tend to describe those who seize opportunities and succeed as "lucky." Luck has nothing to do with how successful entrepreneurs and business leaders do the right things to increase their probability of success. Successful people make their own luck. They ask this question: What can I do to change my situation? When they focus on the possibilities that lie before them instead of what they don't have, they seize control. This control creates success within the opportunity.

Building JRQTV

JRQTV stands for Jon Robert Quinn Television and was originally conceived back in 2008. I was down on my luck and still trying to figure out where to take my life. I was building my motorcycle apparel business online and was kicking the idea around for opening retail stores which I want to get into in the next chapter. I was living at my girlfriend's house and literally had no money.

One day, I had a hair-brain idea to turn a camera on and start filming my life like a reality show and would have the camera in my car and my office and as I would take calls, place orders, ship products, brainstorm, etc, I would be filming and putting the content onto YouTube. This was almost unheard of back in 2008. IRL or In Real Life as they call it today is very common, but back then people thought I was crazy and didn't pay much attention to it.

As I mentioned earlier, JRQTV started as Awepra. Awepra was a "browse engine", very similar to a search engine but instead of searching for what you want, you would browse and the idea was to have everything you wanted or needed within three clicks.

You would visit Awepra.com and if you wanted to shop, you'd click "shop", then if you wanted clothing, you'd click "clothing" and then you'd select your store which were affiliates that generated revenue from shoppers. The concept was great but we were missing one important element which I will get into in a moment.

There are many others ways through which people waste opportunities. They procrastinate. They get lazy. They don't commit. They would rather watch TV than to spend time getting ready for the next opportunity. Instead of watching TV, I started creating TV. To this day, people ask me if I saw this show or that show or did I see the new movie that came out and I always seem out of the loop because I never really got into TV as recreation. I enjoy what goes into building great shows and content, therefore that's where I focus my attention. I have friends that are on hit TV shows, but I've never actually seen the shows.

I have this philosophy that if you want a successful business, you need three important elements. I call this STP - Sustainability, Tenacity and Positioning. How sustainable is your product or design? How much energy does this business take and can you do this for a long period of time? And what is your position in the market or industry? If you're missing even one of those elements, chances are your business will fail. A lot of people confuse opportunity with luck.

They think that having an opportunity means that their lives will change immediately. They think that they will become rich or successful very quickly.

They think of opportunities in the same way as hitting the lottery; that the opportunity will simply get them to their goals with little to no effort on their part.

For example, you might find that there's a good opportunity to start a business and to fill a need in the market. But if you don't go all in and work hard every single day, you really won't make much of your opportunity. In fact, it won't pay off. There are many examples around us of people who conceived of great ideas and went after them only to quit too soon. A few months later, they see their ideas being implemented, and successfully so, by people who truly understand the hard work that takes to grow their business and reap the benefit of their hard work.

So, when looking at Awepra, I had some missing elements. The idea was awesome BUT it wasn't sustainable because the iPhone essentially does the same thing, so why would people want to use my site to do their browsing? It would take WAY too much energy to get enough traffic to the site to generate enough revenue to make the site sustainable, therefore I didn't have enough tenacity to make it work. And position in the market? Apple was already doing the same thing essentially with Apps. This is why businesses fail because they don't understand STP.

When I was approached to build talk shows, I had no idea where my life would go and what would become of it. Awepra was failing and I didn't even know it yet. The talk show business took off like a bat out of hell and I was booking two new guests per week at $500 per guest and had at one point, thirteen advertisers per one hour block. We got to a point where we had so much content, we had to catalog it somehow. There were dozens of shows and we had been filming from day one, so we just started putting everything onto the site and people started referring to it as TV. I was just the guy on the radio filming shows and selling inventory and putting the videos on YouTube and Facebook. I threw the idea out there of Jon Robert Quinn Television and JRQTV which was an idea conceived all those years prior and people loved it. In January 2020, we dropped radio completely along with our billboards and put all of our energy into JRQTV and my greatest achievement was born.

If you are to grow as a leader, you must change with the times. If your company is to expand in the marketplace, it will also need to change to attract new customers. Those who are resistant to change have decided to live with their problems and frustrations rather than face new ones.

The reason is simple: we don't like change because it might mean we'll lose something. Our brain likes to feel comfortable and seeks pleasure over pain. That's why we're tempted to abandon ship at the first sign of distress. Academics call this risk aversion. We feel the pain of loss more acutely than we feel the pleasure of gain. We may like to win, but we hate to lose. Our desire to avoid losses is almost twice as powerful as our desire to take a risk. This explains why we often walk away or fail to seize new opportunities.

Building Retail Stores

I have always had a dream of owning retail stores and in 2011, I made that dream a reality and failed by 2012 leaving me homeless and bankrupt. Do I look at this time of my life as a failure? Absolutely not. Why? Because I learned so much and it made me who I am today.

I was slinging motorcycle helmets and other apparel at flea markets and Craigslist around 2006 and trying to make a name for myself in the music world as a recording artist and guitarist. I've always been a good guitarist but not a great guitarist. I'm good enough to be professional but not good enough to be exceptional. Cutting record after record and only be compared to legends like Joe Satriani and Steve Vai is honourable but when they are saying it's good but not as good as, only limits your career and potential. Selling helmets allowed me to make a living and support my guitar habit.

I've told the story a million times about how I got into helmets and you can reference my other books for that story. This story is about taking the opportunity of opening my retail stores. I had so many helmets coming in and out of my home around 2006, I had no choice but to open a small office. I took an office in a little strip mall in Roseville and found myself being taken serious in the community for riding gear and apparel. There were times that a line formed down the hall and I had no choice but to expand. The opportunity presented itself and I took it. This is where you have to follow intuition. I believe intuition is probably the most important trait in business and only experience gets you this.

If you think of each opportunity as a necessary link to a better one, you will begin to take each small opportunity very seriously. So look at your past actions with maturity, and ask of yourself to do something different. Ask of yourself to do better and to take advantage of the small opportunities even if they don't pay off right away.

After moving into the bigger space, business picked up and I started spending and thinking bigger. I wanted a beautiful store in a mall and my idea was to create a store for men because while women shopped, their men could have a place to hang out. That was the idea. I had two problems. One, I didn't have the money to make this work as I needed it to and two, I didn't understand STP yet and there were missing elements.

I called all three local malls and one wanted something like $6 sqft, the next was around $5 sqft and I went with the cheap alternative of $1.60 sqft. I spent about $30,000 of my own money to build this store, displays, inventory and 45 days later I was out of business. This is called growing too fast, not having intuition and paying for a business education. We can all go to school to learn business but until you're doing it, you don't understand how it actually works.

I took the leap the faith and personally I feel like I won. I learned so much and I know exactly what mistakes not to make next time. Will I ever build another retail store? Probably not. As COVID takes over the world, we're seeing retail die. The entire retail world is different and transforming. Companies that have been around for decades are deteriorating and going bust. Were they missing STP? Well, yes. Their sustainability changed as their position in the market changed.

Buying My Second Harley

I have always loved motorcycles. They have been a part of my life since I was a kid and after getting scared and selling my first Harley, I realized something. I learned another lesson. It wasn't me that I was afraid of or even the traffic, it was the bike. That little Harley 883 was just too small of a bike for the paces of life today with cars in the big city of Sacramento.

Some six or seven months after trading in my first Harley for my wife's SUV for her birthday, I found myself back in a Harley dealer in love with another bike. The problem was this bike I could not afford. Or could I? Here I am making excuses for myself by saying "I can't afford it" rather than "How can I afford it?" My wife was with me and I was talking to the sales guy while she walks up to a 2020 Harley Softail Slim. She comes to me saying, "this is your next bike,"

The salesman looks at me as I start walking the bike and looking at the features. I get on the bike and it feels completely different than the last one. This bike is huge and feels like a Cadillac. He tells me to take it around the block. I keep talking myself out of it saying its too expensive. He hands me the key fob and to tell me what I think. I get on the bike and start it up. After letting out the clutch and it starts to move, then pulling out of the driveway of the dealership, I shift into second, then third. The comfort and transitions between gears and power, I wasn't letting them have their bike back. I get onto the freeway and ride a few miles eventually heading back to the dealer. This bike was almost twice what I wanted to spend on a bike but we made the deal happen. I could have passed on another opportunity and missed the next era of my life. Today, I find myself riding more than driving.

The residual effect of fear is damaging to living a fulfilled, happy and purposeful life. It cripples decision making, hinders success, promotions, finances and the ability to establish long lasting relationships. It generates stress, anxiety and anger and it ultimately leaves you powerless. While fear can subliminally sneak its way into your life, there are key factors to recognize and combat this ugly four-lettered word.

If you notice that you are becoming socially uncomfortable, that you are possessing mixed emotions of anxiety, disappointment, anger, sadness, frustration and regret you may be suffering from fear. But, the first step to every solution is acknowledgement, if you notice fear, bombarding itself into your life, it's time to shift gears and make a change. For me, it was buying my new Harley. I made the decision and it changed my life.

Quit Juggling

I have always had a lot of irons in the fire. At one point I had over fifty online websites selling products because my thought was to have quantity over quality. Well, where did that get me? Bankrupt. The lesson? Focus.

I must be honest — I'm talking to myself here. For most of my life, I've been moving from one opportunity to the other. That changed about ten years ago then I decided to only focus on growing JRQTV and incorporating everything I was currently working on and bringing all of my past projects into one place.

For many years, I had too many priorities and zero focus. It was time for me to rethink my opportunities. However, it's never a matter of finding opportunities. Everyone has opportunities. So it's not about how many opportunities you have, it's about how many opportunities you eliminate from your life and quit juggling. I see so many small business owners that want to be an overnight success and they are bouncing from one thing to another and become a jack of all trades. As I get older, I find myself doing less and less and that can be looked at two ways depending on your mindset. You could see it as I'm getting lazy or that I am getting more comfortable with my craft and putting quality into my work.

I had to make a choice. When you go to the circus, you see the juggler with four or five or even six balls and it sure is a sight to see. There comes a point where he's now got seven, then eight, then nine and when he drops one, he drops everything and in the business world, that's called a game over. I decided to only focus on my books, music, and JRQTV. Why? Because, they all complement each other and I realized it was time to focus on quality over quantity.

Something I get asked a lot is how I get so much work done. It always makes me smile when people ask me this as I often think that I could (and maybe should) be doing a lot more than I do. Something that I have been experimenting with this year though is not working on too many projects at once and not being afraid to say something will have to wait until next month. In fact I usually try to work on one main project at a time and schedule other things after that project has finished.

My day usually starts with me waking up naturally. I usually only schedule one appointment per day and usually after 11am so I can enjoy my morning. I am usually out of bed by 9am and walk the dog. Then I will take a shower and hop on the bike (Harley) and get Starbucks. I get back to the house in time to head to my meeting by 11am and then around 1pm, I am usually done for the day. I can spend the rest of day working on budgets, creating new products or thinking. I do more thinking than actual work these days. If I can film one new project a week and release one new intellectual property per month, such as a new book or new music, then I am staying productive and creating more wealth for myself. I do not do anything for my business that does not generate revenue.

So many small business owners create products and services and don't think about ROI (return on investment) and though creating intellectual properties only generate a couple of dollars or even just a few cents, when in volume, it creates generational wealth and in my opinion it's way better than real estate because there is virtually no risk. I can create music and get paid for the rest of my life from it. The same with books. I can write a book and it sells and the more I create, the more money I make for myself. This folks, is how people get rich.

Sure Why The Hell Not

As I conclude this book, I think about the title I chose for this book and wonder if it's the right title. Then it comes to me, Sure, Why the Hell Not! If this book makes it to the best sellers list, then great. If it doesn't, then oh well. Why? Because even if one person gets something from this book, it's a success. This book is short and sweet but intended to provide value to those who need the inspiration needed to better their lives and honestly, all success stories start by telling yourself. Sure, Why the Hell Not.

When I met my wife in front of a Starbucks one night in January 2013, I never thought in a million years, we'd be married one day. She told me years later she wasn't sure she wanted to even meet me. She said I was kind of a dick and didn't like me too much but she had nothing going on so she literally said, "Sure, why the hell not". Now we're married.

At the end of the day, an opportunity is just a chance of making something good happen. An opportunity alone means nothing. Give ten people the same opportunity, and you'll get ten different outcomes.

Our world is a weird place and life is crazy and without adventure we have nothing. Just remember, you only live once. Look, life is full of opportunity. You just have to figure out which opportunities you're going after. And yes, that's a hard thing to figure out. You also don't control the opportunities that come your way. What do you control? How prepared you are. So stop chasing everything like a happy dog in the park on a summer day. Just keep things simple, work on your skills, character, and become better at a few things every single day.